STRAIGHT AHEAD

Clare Shaw was born in Burnley in 1972. She has published three collections with Bloodaxe, *Straight Ahead* (2006), which was shortlisted for the Glen Dimplex New Writers' Award for Poetry and attracted a Forward Prize Highly Commended for Best Single Poem; *Head On* (2012), which according to the *Times Literary Supplement* is 'fierce, memorable and visceral'; and her latest collection, *Flood* (2018).

She is a Royal Literary Fellow, and a regular tutor for the Writing Project, the Poetry School, the Wordsworth Trust and the Arvon Foundation. She also works as a mental health trainer and consultant and has taught and published widely in the field, including *Our Encounters with Self-Injury* (eds. Baker, Biley and Shaw, PCCS 2013) and *Otis Doesn't Scratch* (PCCS 2015), a unique storybook resource for children who live with self-injury.

Clare lives in Hebden Bridge with her daughter and their two pet rats; she enjoys rock climbing and wild swimming in cold and beautiful places.

CLARE SHAW

STRAIGHT AHEAD

BLOODAXE BOOKS

ISBN: 978 1 85224 750 8

First published 2006 by
Bloodaxe Books Ltd,
Eastburn,
South Park,
Hexham,
Northumberland NE46 1BS.

www.bloodaxebooks.com

For further information about Bloodaxe titles
please visit our website and join our mailing list
or write to the above address for a catalogue.

Supported using public funding by
ARTS COUNCIL
ENGLAND

Cover design: Neil Astley & Pamela Robertson-Pearce.

Digital reprint of the 2006 Bloodaxe Books edition.

ACKNOWLEDGEMENTS

Acknowledgements are due to the editors of the following publications where versions of some of these poems first appeared: *Nerve*, *Poetry Life*, and the *Writer's Inc Writers of the Year Anthology* (2003).

'Foreign Tastes' was first published in *Out of Fashion, an anthology of poems*, edited by Carol Ann Duffy (Faber, 2004).

Thanks are due to the Arvon and Jerwood Foundations for their support in the form of the Arvon/Jerwood Young Writer's Award 2003/2004.

And thanks for all the support and encouragement I've received, especially from George Szirtes, Jackie Kay and Carol Ann Duffy, and from my friends.

CONTENTS

Not as simple

It's not as simple as growing up
and looking back, telling a story
that leads from one event to the next.

Neither is it as simple
as going in circles. That would imply
a going. Instead,

it's like certain landscapes, a mixture of map and geology,
of prehistoric and industrial history.
And also, it is biology,

as well as being the strange light
at an unspecifiable time of the day
in unseasonable weather, the wrong country.

But no, it is not so simple as being lost
or even finding your way on your knees
by darkness.

It is not so simple as ears,
mouths, your ears, my
mouth. It is similar to fingers,

though nothing like that. You get me?
It is miscellaneous, only
much more complex.

It is English characters in Welsh soap operas
screened in Germany.
It will never make any sense

or turn out right in the end. It is just
not as simple as doing your best
or getting the general gist, oh no,

not as simple as painting or writing
or any form of telling or saying, of laying
the right words in just the right order. Just

look at me trying.

Poem for a bus shelter

This is not a life, but if it were
I'd say I always lived here.
I'd say this street; this long grey face
of factories, flats; the boarded shops;
the tired, concrete houses, squats –
they saw my first bright day.

I was clean as a breeze,
as cold as glass. I sweated rain,
was slicked by the wind, was beautifully bare.
I filled myself with city sound,
the blur and swirl of good blue air.

When winter came, and the gale,
and the church roof flapped and fractured like a wing;
when thin trees fell
and shop-fronts swelled and bellied –
I stood my ground.

I knew where I belonged.
I was the colour of a dockside warehouse,
blue-grey. The shade of a cold,
an evening cloud, a hangover, a foggy day.
If I had ever had a life

I would say that I was proud
and it could be true.
Come rain or snow,
come the long white corridor
of Christmas;

come crowds with spiteful corners; come
the wet green growl of winter spit;
come fist; come kick;
come the lurch of stolen cars;
come stone; come brick;
come *I luv Gaz, Mick,*

Shaz; come weekend chips;
come drunken piss; come empty cans;
come the sad pink skins of condoms,
dog shit, sick –

come morning, I was there.

And if I had ever had a life
half worth the privilege of the name –
if I had not been rooted to this spot
and treated to the things
that other lives spit out

I would be proud
and I would write it –
I would write it clear and loud
in bold black ink
with my bold black hand
I would write it.

I woz ere.

This baby

This baby is a hurricane –
it's the thunder of an underground train.
You can hear it coming from miles away.
You can feel it in the walls, the floor.

It's the roar beneath the city street;
the earthquake that wakes you,
shaking beds, breaking plates.
This baby dislodges slates –

felled a steeple in Dudley.
This baby could kill.

This baby is news, big news.
This baby makes you huge.
Makes you Africa and Russia,
proud. A high hot-air balloon fat-filled with fire.

You could explode with it.
Stand clear! This woman could blow any minute!

*

This quick blood-bloom of certain cells
could grow to anything -
snowflakes forming like wildflower
a sly-eyed gull; a dinosaur;

a deep-green bellyful of weed.
This baby is a fallen seed.
The thin grass blade that ruptures the road.
It could open you up –

your stomach, the shape of a book not yet written;
the curve of the first word
of the page you wake speaking,
always forgotten.

It's like that, this baby —
the light of a star that no-one can see
travelling ten thousand light years
to catch you unaware

knelt as you are in the slow Autumn rain,
heaving with dreams
and your body a poem
on the theme of 'This Baby'.

Think of a name.

The year Dad left

was summer, the year that the ladybird plague
had marbled the yard with hot red shells.
Tar melted between the cobbles
and we went barefoot till our soles grew hard.

On telly, volcanoes flowed like something you could eat.
Ingots looked chewable. Switched off,
the screen gave a soft electric breath.
For what we are about to receive.

In the old-man smell of Mass,
women sang like chickens would, tinny and shrill.
And Lord, I was thankful
for my sister's zip-up anorak

for *Look and Learn* and *Star Trek*,
for the balloon that reached Australia.
For 'Clare's writing is a pleasure'.
For coming third

in the Burnley Silver Jubilee Parade.
Sherbet made stars on the roof of my mouth
and I painted the Queen beneath the banner of a rainbow
in a castle like a Christmas cracker hat.

Crackerjack! All summer, Miss Snell walked in circles
and the girl with Down's from off the estate
came up with her mother.
In our back yard, Action Men fell and died

bleeding bright felt-tip that wouldn't wash out.
It was a royal year, right? Each night,
the warm sheet of my mother's cheek.
God bless. The miles-off sound of voices,

careless, the way that children are.
Careless: as if they couldn't care less.

Foreign tastes

Claudine and you pretended a crush
on the boys in Class Seven.
You were David, pucker-mouthed.

You practised kissing on the bed.
Claudine was thin and bitey
like one of Alan's ferrets

but her mother was an angel-fish;
an eyelash flash of blue
and sun-tan orange

with the leopard-skin glamour
of a holiday brochure.
Her house was packed with fat, gold furniture,

waist-high tigers
and bingo-prize buddhas.
A warm aquarium gargled in the corner

and Shirley Bassey sang loud enough
to break a law.
This, your tight-permed mother said,

was because she was foreign
and had unusual tastes.
You thought about this

after dark, imagined
she'd taste of coconut
and stolen rum,

the tight-throat burn of cigarettes,
hot mud, midnight swimming
and somewhere a long way from Burnley.

And after you were kissed goodnight
you'd stroke your rib-striped chest,
think of foreign things.

Mrs O'Hara

read the same two books each year
to a different class.
When she reached the end,
we watched her cry like grandparents would,
baffled and concerned,
then turned to other things. Sunshine. Dust.

How the tops of the desks were grained like snails;
how your breath could set up a mist
for your name to pool in.
The soft lines of a pencil in varnish,
the hairs on a wrist.

I remember best
how I was first in everything
that year, how much she loved
my writing, how words fell from me then
like a new animal walking.

We learned our first thin rules with her,
the full stops and the capitals.
You do not start with 'And' or 'But'.
A word should not appear in a sentence twice.
You never use a word as weak as 'nice'
except for biscuits.

She taught another word for blue,
it was 'azure'
where the clouds frayed, billowy.
Sent us home with a mouthful of dictionary;
a bright new word for every story.

In spring, Salvo's postcard came from Sicily,
full of new school
and the sun in the azure blue sky.

Days passed and passed
and the huge year rolled towards summer.
Mrs O'Hara turned the last pages

on *I Am David* and *The Silver Sword*.
Another class.

Mrs O'Hara,
there are things I still remember.
The smell of lemon and polished wood.
The three o'clock walk home.
Gravel and weeds and fights by the stream.
The voices like seagulls, high and loud.
A fraying sky.
An azure cloud.

How to demolish a house

Start with the swing and the slide,
hide the miniature cars and
the trike with the squeak.

Bury the gnome.
rip the ivy out from the brick,
cut the hedge right back

to its root. Strip all the fruit from the tree.
Open the door to the greenhouse.
Wait for frost.

Pick a fistful of stones.
Take out the birds at the table
one by one.

Cut down the lines to the phone.
Scrape off the name
from its plate. *Dunrovin.*

Erect a high fence to deter intervention.
Dig out the foundation. Observe
the slump of the roof like tarpaulin.

How the rain pools
where the cat used to watch in the morning.
Plough up the garden.

Ignore the old bones, the pink panic
of worms. Step across
the limp grey felt of the moles.

Now the black crows rise
like bad news.
Steal the spare keys.

Don't make a noise. Avoid

the tangle of boots in the hallway.
The shadows of coats on their hooks.

Now place a small bomb.
Don't mention a thing.
Don't warn anyone.

I'll give you something to cry about

Slap.
Your nose is a broken tap. Drip. Drip.
You could be sick
with the size of the fear in your throat.
His drumming fingers. The slow count:
one – two – three

Slap.
Each word is a loud red shout
across your arms your legs your face.
You know the script:
you're a bad lad, fact.

You're a bad lad.
Watch the sharp, white storm of words
that swerve and spiral past your ears.
Bad lad. *Watch them float*

a smoke-swirl, out into the sky
that shimmers bluer than a pool
above the shoulders
of the shape in front of you.

Slap.
You've read about it – being shot
can feel like a fist. The shock.
The sudden, blunt heat.
You think of this, hard.

Picture yourself in your cowboy suit.
You see yourself tall at the OK Corral.
The hero, fallen.
Tumbleweeds roll.
Clint Eastwood whistles something lonely.

Bright-frilled women weep in bars.
There is no pain.
John Wayne is leaning over you.
'Goodbye,' you say.
His face is soft and sad and

Thud.
All the lights you ever saw
are glaring in your head;
the roar, the gun-sharp taste of blood.
'I'll goodbye you, my lad!'

and you're pulled by the hair so fast
your feet are a drumroll on the stairs
and you swear swear swear
so hard it makes your teeth ache
that whatever it costs

you'll be bigger than this.
Whatever it takes
you'll be big.

Sunday roast. You watch
the snowfall of language around you
how it settles, white
on the cabbage and meat.

Eat up and grow up
big like your Dad.
The hard rind sticks in your throat
like bait.

Nothing personal,

you just had something he wanted.
He had a plan
and you wandered in. You fitted,

tall for your age (ten).
Think of it like this – you were
a prop in a play, a walk-on part,

you were meat. Live weight.
Small fish on a hook
with the smell of the morning lake still on you.

How you rode right up
on your silver-blue, nearly-new bike. Bad luck.
Bad egg that he wanted to crack.

You were
a wonderful drug, good
like smashing a car, like starting a fire

or a war. A beautiful plate.
An exercise mat. Convenient site.
Bright light that he wanted

out. You were incidental,
nothing personal. A young animal,
a small event in the shape of a girl.

He couldn't be bothered
to hate you. Didn't kill you. Felt
close to you in the end.

Walked away warm with the sense
that today
he did something kind.

Summer holiday

I

The green-gold summers ended
with that first long road into August;
the car packed high as a hiker;
four elbow-tight kids in the back.
Minutes from home, the singing would stop

and the night would set in.
Then the motorway drone down to Dover,
the orange-grey flat;
the waiting-room whiteness of service stations;
the bright rash of warehouse, estate.

Marking the distance with coffee and Coke.
The syrup-thick stereo soundtrack.
Feeling homesick.
Feeling sick.
The morning stained yellow with smoke.

II

Down the low road to the shore,
the sharp regiments of tents,
the angry sand.
The shattered glass of pine and bracken.
The high, unbroken crowd of children,

quick as the striped-tail flick
of the lizard on the cracked red wall.
The clockwork birdsong
of crickets, whirring.

The wide night, bright as an eye.
Deep. Silver-sleepless and hot.
The stale leather smell of sweat.
Drip.

Drip.

Matchhead-red,
the tent walls shake
with every breath.
Slow drumroll of the zip.
Tick.
Tick.

Everything
is coming
awake.

III

Imagine you are fifteen.
You are trying on
the strange new shape of your body.
Short skirt, tight top.
Imagine. You might be a gift, bright wrapped.

Imagine you are fifteen.
The darkened bar
is the smell of a late night city.
There is no sound for the shape you are in.
All your words are seagulls
in the loud blue sky.

Imagine you are fifteen and
you are a limp white fish on the shore
and your mouth is rounding out
the long low 'O' of drowning.

You are fifteen.
He is thirty-eight.
Imagine.
Foregone conclusion.

IV

Penguin Popular Reference Spanish Phrasebook 1978

Call a doctor.

There has been an accident.
A girl is badly hurt.

How old is she?
What is her name?

My name is __
I am __ years old.

I have burned/cut/bruised myself.
I can't sleep/eat.
Do you understand me?

I want to have these things washed.
What will it cost?

Are you willing to act as a witness?

Breathe in.
Breathe out.
Does that hurt?

V

At the next day market
they broke a duck's neck
in front of you. Quack-quack
Snap. You didn't feel a thing.

Ya-uuk

Seven year old orang-utan. Rescued from zoo. Sucks thumb.

Place of rain and light and the sky full of life
as the earth that squirmed in the mouth
and the sharp red ants like a stream of bites

and the weight of my mother's breast on my face,
the hot white taste
and the chase through the trees and the cries,

the rake of the sun on my back
and the crack of the air like a full nut, breaking,
the long wet night and the cat.

I knew it, and the sound of the feet,
and the sting of the smoke.
The man with his breath like rotten meat.
His sour white skin and his gun.

And the shake and the choke of the track,
the sharp stones flying, the voices shouting,
the cut of the bars that sliced the light,
the hard black sky and no rain.

How the trees ran away like water
and the air was a river poured over my mouth
so I couldn't breathe and I couldn't get out
and a dark thing boiled inside me

like everything died before it was dead
and the floor was hard and the food was bone
and we slept and we dreamed of the leaves and the sun
and we slept and we dreamed we were dead.

Now world is the cold pink stink of a man
and all of the outside is gone.

My name is Ya-uuk.

I was taken from sun. I was flung on a truck.
Now I suck and I bite and I rock
myself; I rock and I bite and I suck.

Poem about Dee Dee

I

Dee Dee is out on the hospital roof.
From here, Liverpool is a story
she can read from beginning to end.

If you've never driven too fast
into a bend in the road,
felt the slow slide of your stomach

into a corner of itself;
if you've never leaned back
at the top of a rock,

felt the knot of the rope
like a waking snake
squirm loose in your hand;

if you've never walked home to a lover,
your tongue like a blade in your throat
to tell her it's over;

if you've never known
the milk-white explosion
of a moment that could last forever;

then you have no idea how she felt.

II

Just one short sprint of thirty feet
to the low grey wall
and the city laid out like a map of itself.

Close your eyes
and it's Sports Day.
You can smell the new-cut field.

There's a crowd of everyone, bright
as if they'd been dipped in the river.
Everyone there you'd want to be there

and the sound of the cheer
is your big day out; it's the prom
and the beer; the kiss under the Tower;

it's a Midnight Mass of drunken song
and you're pounding the pitch
to the finishing line

to be first to the faces waiting there;
the waiting arms,
the waiting air.

III

Two guards and three nurses
bring her down.

It's evening, lock-up
and you're drinking your tea
watching the hours
drain in the grey outside.

You see the streaks of concrete
on her face
and you remember the weight
of a grown man balled

through the fist
of his knees in your back.
You remember the taste,
like molten rust.

You remember your arms
pushed to the back of your neck;
how your shoulders were a flame
that scorched your chest

until all it could hold

was a necklace of tiny, red gasps.

You remember when
all that you were
was a scream
that no one could hear.

IV

The day room is a late-night
fish tank of sound
and yellow shadow.
The hum, bang, clatter of the ward.

Dormitories simmer with sleep.
I am wide-eyed with two weeks awake.
Her eyes
are methadone-heavy.

We watch TV in the small hours,
eating Frosties dry from the box.
We know all the tunes to Ceefax,
baiting the glaze-eyed agency staff

with high-risk jokes.
'How about a day out?
It's been three months since I crossed a road
and I'm beginning to lose the knack.'

Dee Dee and me are having a laugh
dreaming plans for O.T. –
rock climbing schemes
for the deeply depressed.

A barebacked parachute jump.
A Blackpool trip. Imagine
riding the Big One
with your seatbelt undone.

Dee Dee laughs.
Feels the wind in her hair,
the world spinning its pages
beneath her.

God, we laughed,
in there
you could die laughing

This is a true story

It was just before one when she rang
and I picked up the phone to hear
'Clare, our plane has gone down
somewhere right of the Isle of Man.'
'Are you dead then?' I said. Down the wire,

a sound like the roar of a crowd
then my sister's laugh and her cough. 'I'm alive.
When we fell from the sky to the sea
it was grey, it looked calm. There was one low cloud,
its shadow thrown off to the left,

a long arm of land I can't see any more.
As we got near, the waves were like tarmac
under the wheels of a car. Then a shock
the size of my body, but bigger
like a brick clapped hard either side of my head.
I didn't expect all this pain.

But now that I'm in it,
beyond all prospect of help or return
I have to admit there's something about it,
my feet hung over this deep new world
like I'm all root, or as near as a person can be to flight,
or a wick in a candle that hasn't been lit,

there's creatures beneath me
have never been named.' And I thought,
there's so much to learn from my sister,
her good clean strength and her grit.
The receiver grew sticky and wet
like blood.

And then it was still.
The cry of a single gull.
The soot-black blast of a ship's foghorn.

Gone. I was two hours stood

with my ear to that phone.

And when I think of my sister,
her fear of deep water
and all her hard work and her hope, I could weep.
I could sit down here and just give up.
I feel like just giving up.

Love poem

As it got later, you got drunker
and I loved you more than ever as
your words formed noisy queues
that wouldn't wait,
broke out in fights and took short cuts.
They tripped each other up.
Fresh thoughts spun from you, loud and bright
as children from a water slide.
I was awed by you, afraid of you,
like you were juggling fire or blades.

And I loved you more than ever when we left
and the fresh air hit you like another pint.
You were blurred and way too dignified,
walked into glass that wasn't there
and wandered like a lost balloon.
Your face was slow and moony
like cows are, blank as a plate.
Your voice made faint paths
that your words stumbled after
and never came back.

I made sense of the pavement for you –
could walk, and that was enough for you.
Solemn and precarious,
you dragged from my shoulders
like a bag of Sunday papers.
Threw up noisily by the lock
where geese came creaking from their sleep,
their long mouths open like night flowers.
A wise move, I told you. You were
too far gone to bother,
smelt of compost heap, hot weather.

I got you home and undressed.
You were damp and irrational

like after sex.
In bed, your sudden stillness scared me.
I wanted to count your breathing all night
but instead, I slept
until you woke mustily
as though in a tent on a hot early morning
taken aback by the humming of summer,
the sudden blue sun.

Oh my love is like a red, red rose
that's newly sprung in June.

War poem

I'm half absent, putting
milk in the bin
when War walks in,
trailing her slippers.

It's coffee she wants, and quickly.

In the corner, Radio Four
talks to the air
like a lost woman
in a dressing-gown.

War has plans for today:
I'm briefed over breakfast,
a tick list of tasks
portioned out with precision.

If the weather permits, War will start
with the garden, wrestling weeds
and the tall lawn
which has argued itself to knee height.

War is edgy,
complains of an ache
which nothing to do
with last night's red wine.

By mid-afternoon,
War is soaked with frustration.
The mower lacks
a certain piece of plastic

without which, War
can only mow in circles.
War is ploughing a spiral trough
of mud and savaged turf.

War sighs, washes her hands
of the whole blown mess.
Takes a drive into town.
List in hand, she's set-eyed.

Precise. Tick-tick.
Job done,
cuts a quick line home
in the brown Pennine rain.

The road's loud gravel.
I hear her return like a storm,
heave herself, bagged,
through the door.

Tonight, it's just the two of us –
me and War,
guarding the dark
with whiskey and fire.

Sound down,
the television flickers grey.
War leans heavy against me,
breathing slows to a slur.

Lights off, soft, in the kitchen.

Radio Four
continues its insistence
to the air:
this is war this is war this is war.

In Bedfordshire, the rivers rise

In Bedfordshire, the rivers rise
and flood in flat black plains
of rapid mud. I'm driving
to a climb. The rain

in rusted run-off from the hills,
gathers, swells in muddy pools
that twist the steering-wheel.
I form a fist

and grip until my hands turn white,
our argument still wet and sour
inside my mouth.
I'm listening to Radio Four –

the price of oil and votes and fish and war
(I grip until my hands turn numb)
and how the rivers rise down south
and colder days are yet to come.

Cold. My hands against the rock,
I fold a palm around a hook
and heave towards the top and drop.
My arms swing like a drunken ape.

I stop, drink coffee,
hear how last year's flood defences hold.
I think of sandbags, think of
ringing her, decide on
Not. Decide a new route up the rock

and ropeless, climb five times
above the limit of my head.
At thirty foot, my legs shake
like I'm spinning thread.
The wall leans back.

I think of it – the sudden fall,
the long blue shock,
the whole kick of my body
on the rock. I call and call
and warn her

of the flooding fields in Bedfordshire;
the swelling pools that twist and steer;
the rapid mud, the tightened fist.
The things that fear can make you do.
The lengths that fear can drive you to.

I grip until my hands turn numb.
Listen now. I'm telling you –
the coldest days are yet to come.
Dark rain is straining at the skies
and rivers rise, and rise, and rise.

London – Todmorden

This journey started in London
in argument
and it just got worse from there.

I slept in a bed too short for my body.
All night, the drink kept me restless
until morning came yellow,
smelling of traffic and smoke. I was sick.

We woke ourselves by drinking
Coke. The green-brown Thames
was thick as a broth
with all manner of things

and the sky was the colour of falling
when we started for home.
We argued before we reached the train.
I sat in a different carriage.

Your face was a door
slammed hard.
The football crowd boarded in Runcorn
and there was nothing left to read.

I wish I could go back.
There were some things I wanted I left there
like the hour watching the river
frowning light; the black

shock of your body like water.
The short bed, the long night.

It's Saturday evening.
The Todmorden train.
Smaller, darker.
The usual rain.

Maybe somewhere

You wake with each lover you left,
morning sun and the air hung with dust.
Maybe somewhere, all the lives you could have lived
are still going on; shops, work,
a patch of garden, the usual things.
Early evenings soft with voices,
the small gestures you learned to forget.

The houses you could have lived in.
A woman takes down a pan from a high shelf
as a child you should have known
rides on your shin to a song
that would have driven you mad
if you'd heard it. Again and again.

Maybe somewhere, a world
where everything you did is still undone,
and what you broke, made right.
The night you turned into a knife to cut yourself
stays mild as a shut mouth,
the same trees speaking like water.

You miss them now,
the languages you can't remember
as you walk through these different rooms
quite breathless with regret.
You carry your heart like a stiff fish. Gutted.
And all day, you hear their faces echoing,
how they looked at you as you left.

A sudden corner to this cold house.
Its empty rooms and its silence. The unmoved air.
The voices you can't recall anymore.
In the darkness, the cruel liquid sound
of the wind and the trees.
All of them, all of them, calling you fool.

About the arguments we had last year

It would have been so easily ended
back then,
the three hour arguments
that left us shaking,

the urgent late night drive,
two other cars on the road
between here and North Yorkshire,
the yellow-grey hedgerows,

the sudden open page
of an owl lifting, and all the way
the right words
and none of them good enough.
My chest was a jar full of fishes
that couldn't get air.

Without you, everything fell.
Trees rotted soft; the snow melted
and the paths stank.
Words could not speak themselves,
familiar places did not
know me anymore.

That night,
Settle was black with sleep
and empty. There was
a single bleat from the hill.
We lay still in the bed
and your skin was cold.

I remember all that
and spend a minute now
imagining
it was over last year and yet
here you are

and the moment comes heavy with light
and dripping, your face
close to sleep and smiling.
Our ordinary bed,
the same song playing

and you,
a candle behind each eyelid,
a fat apple landed
where it was least expected.
Extraordinary,

like a leopard walked in, glowing
from the wet night
on Back Commercial Street,
to lay with me, breaking

all known barriers of reason and place
to be with me.

Straight ahead

is the back of the seat,
a lump of gum at its metal trim
and the long blonde hair
of the woman in front. I'm wearing
my thick black coat

too hot, so I pull down the zip
and the air on my throat
is a shock – like being touched.
I can smell myself, an old house
that no one lives in, someone died in,

choky, dark. There's a lot to cover up –
I'm wide shoulders, a back
you could break on, an old door
you can't get open. I swear sometimes
I can hear myself creak.

Two seats back, the sound of a Walkman.
It reminds me of something –
a night in a bar, the smell of a woman
with long blonde hair,
the sound of the windmills up on the moor.

It's a clear blue day with a bite,
the sun showing everything up
like flecks on bricks.
It makes me feel awake
the way that pain does.

When I put my hand to the back of her seat
I say sorry to no one in particular.
She looks at me and I wish
my coat was done up a bit higher.
I can feel the weight

of my glasses on my face. I smell
like someone's breath in the morning
after a night of committed drinking.
I smell like an eye that can't see too well.
I'm sat like a closed-up book,

I've an ache in my neck. The woman in front
smells sweet of fruit,
a red smell you could climb into
and never get out; a great, wet
nest of a smell, a sudden huge bloom

and I'm sat with my head tipped back
and my eyes half shut
just sniffing it up. A taste of blood
like my body burst into my mouth,
too big for itself. A smell of smoke,
the same music from two seats back.

I can still see her
I can still see her
how she pulls up the car at night on the moor
just to hear
those big white windmills slicing the air.

Plucked

And if your right eye should offend against you, then pluck it out.
MATTHEW 5:29

It did offend. It held
a snapshot of her in her new black top;
the row of deliberate
holes down the back. How I touched
the tip of my finger to her spine.

So it had to be plucked.
The muscles gripped
in a long hot blink; the nerve unravelled,
a ragged cord. Everywhere it seemed,
the slick gel that smelt
of nothing; the metal sting of the air
where nothing was.

And worse. I'd think of her,
the crisp curl of her rising between my thighs.
I was wet as light all over.
Alone, just the dull cat watching
on an empty afternoon.
I'd say her name
because there had to be a sound
to go with this – the cold shame
of my own right hand, and my bad mind
with the wrong face in it,
her face, blazing.

It wasn't like you'd expect.
It was meat. It was
yellow and greasy. Blisters of fat.
I was technical, rhythmic,
right down to the bone.

And so on. The criminal skin
which rippled like a blown field
when she was around – all gone.
Exposed,
the nerves were a squabble
of first violins.

And the feet that walked to her door,
the ears like two stuck records
repeating her words.
All were removed.
A sharp surface wore a clump of hair
that had been brushed for her;
a tooth that had shone in a smile for her.
The spongy lungs. My tongue
was surprisingly long when uprooted.

Soon nothing remained
but a stained ridge of flint
in the form of a fibula; the wicked flower
of a heart.

Undressed of its flesh and helpless,
in a bloody mess of its making.
No words, no sight, no nothing,
just its bucking and its shuddering,
its mindless repeating.
And no matter what, it kept on loving
and hurting and hating and beating.

A poem about babies

I showed you a poem about babies
and wrote one; tried to describe
my sister's latest son, the way
his far gaze followed the light.
How, on his first day,
I was a tall wall he leaned on,
a curved cave he could lie inside
and as weeks went on
with him, they were yellow and screaming.
I wanted you to see him laughing,
whatever it was that made him dance.
You wouldn't come.

So I blushed around pregnant women,
the danger and distance of them,
all seedy with flesh and waiting,
a plump-globed, loose-lipped pendulum
I couldn't place. I thought of them
stripey and warm like badgers,
the full drum of them sounding in my bed.
When I put my head to your stomach,
nothing spoke.

We talked of holidays we never took
and one night, I dreamt of a daughter,
a swollen pain like a plum.
She was blonde as an ingot,
and sturdy. Her face was a hook
and it cut me. She looked
as though she knew me.
When I woke up, you had gone.

At least a dream is only a dream,
as you said, quite rational to the last.
It is an utter waste of time
to miss someone who can't be there.

Today I saw
my brother's seventh child,
one week old, plump and curled.
Her eyebrows, ledged
like his are; his thick blond hair.
She was breathing like
a cat does, sleeping;
a faint and regular popping and creaking.
The quiet sound of a bubble exploding.
Unbearably empty air.

Killing it

It didn't want to die. When we starved it,
it just thought of happier times,
crept back in its mind and stared at us
as if it didn't know us any more.

At night,
it rocked itself, a slow ship,
a young monkey with a brick
and no mother.

Onlookers were full of compliments,
looked to us for guidance.
We told them about the taste of wine
by a high stone church in Spain

while under the table
we stamped on it as we spoke.
Made it live by rules
that we changed and broke at a whim.

Ashamed, we hated it
for making us both so cruel.
Would not speak to or about it;
would not give it the most basic of things.

Denied it air,
kept the door tight shut on it.
It licked sunshine from the windows
like rain

and did not complain
as you, so gentle and thin,
turned your back on it.
The shadow of light on your spine.

I started it. Threw a cup at it,

and you, a random ornament.
Then it was plates and books, it was
upped to a sudden push
and it was sprawled on the floor,
the damp clump of a boot in a gut.

And how we shook it:
the small bones of its skull
tinkled like mirrors; its eyes were
robotic with horror.

I may have stirred to a single inaudible word
that night; you may have caught
the sound of its breath;
a loose cough, nothing poetic.

Either way,
neither of us noticed its death.

Until we woke to it,
blue-lipped and smelling of mould.
Solidly cold.

White-faced, we looked at each other
aghast, new strangers.
There's nothing alive left between us.

In Halifax,

a mother, two boys and a daughter get on.
They sit over the aisle from me.
The girl is maybe three years old.
She swings between the tables
and the mother says Stop it or you'll fall.
She carries on swinging anyway and falls.
It's Thursday.

I'm reading a new book,
the same line again and again.
Their noise distracts me.
They're discussing whether I'm a woman or a man.
At Bradford, a man and a woman get on.
They sit opposite me.

A group of Spanish students take photos of each other
and the girl joins in. The mother says
Asylum seekers they're out for everything they can get
and the man says I'm with you on that.
I try not to listen but I can't help it.
New Pudsey.

The mother and children get off and the man says
Kids I love them, and I say
They're all right until they're thirteen
and try to carry on reading
but he's determined and tells me
they've been away this weekend,

his girlfriend's first time on a train
and she liked it. He likes the coach, used to drive one
until they took his licence. I say
Haven't you had enough of coaches then?
and he says No and looks sad for a bit
and tells me they're out for a curry tonight.

In Leeds, we walk to the bus stop,
one of those long yellow buses that bends in the middle
and I go where I'm going.
For some reason I can't stop laughing.
By five, the day is darkening. The traffic is heavy
and most cars have their lights on.

When I walked to the station this morning
sheep watched from the ridge and the sun lit up
the pocked grey crags on the moor,
a blackbird pecking the wall, dust falling.
Cold evening, and a feeling

like there isn't one person can hold all this,
not a shout loud enough or swear word
hard enough, no stunned slapped sound
or person strong enough or big enough, no knocked
from one thing to another woman tall enough

not the sea or the night sky
with all its silence and light; that space
and not one answer
anywhere.

It's a cold night now.
There's one large star.
I fill in a British Rail questionnaire, say
General cleanliness –
very poor.

Hope

It's not good for me, this hope.
It makes a snake of my guts. I can hardly walk
for the hissing in my stomach.
My chest is a slow explosion;
my head is a high-domed cathedral
packed with children. Everything I do
is an act of expectation.

It makes a fool of me, this hope.
It has me reading signs in smoke,
the direction taken by traffic, rain,
the quick shapes of the starlings in flock. It tells me
that if I walk to the end of the street
without stepping on a crack,
if I drink from the opposite lip of the cup –
I say 'please' to no one in particular
about a thousand times a day

and remind myself of each reason
why it won't happen, the odds are impossibly low.
While all the time, the hope is scanning shop-windows
for unbelievably small shoes. Walking in,
I catch myself in the mirror, hopeful, famous,
luminous as a sick child or a saint.
My mouth is a word beginning to happen,
my smile is a joke I can't tell anyone.
I'm enigmatic as a head-girl,
prim with secrets, unusually clean. My eyes shine
like two framed awards for trying hard,
I feel like patting myself on the head.

This hope is a small black dog
and it won't stop jumping up. However I try,
I can't get rid of it. I think I've left it behind
when suddenly, thud – I'm on my knees in the park
begging the dizzying sky.

And sometimes I wish I could kill it.
Locate the exact point where it lives in my chest
and drive in a stake. But the hope won't die.
I drown it in beer and it laps it up,
starts singing and dancing, beaming, telling
taller and louder tales, till I can see it all,

believe it all, quite feasible and real,
I can smell it, touch it,
right down to the grain of the table, the coffee,
the curve of the light on an apple,
the slow stewing of water in a sunlit vase,
the smell of warm flowers.
The random sounds of my lover upstairs.
The ache in my shoulders. My baby's face.

For you

I would consider killing
a large insect, a sick animal, sometimes
one or two bad people
all to make you a space. I have at least

thirteen spare hours a week; I don't need
to sleep so much, eat so much.
I'll grow small for you, we'll share
a seat. No one need even notice

you're here. How many stars
burn out each night, leaving a gap
the size of a world?
Billions of stars like rain.

It is spring, new things
recklessly claiming life
wherever I walk, blossom
displaying itself to the sky.

Inevitable that someone will die,
is dying right now, and a space happens.
I want you to slip in quickly,
even if it isn't your turn.

Some questions

Why is fire? Why is fire
hot like being shouted at,
a tiny star? Why fire like
a fruit you shouldn't eat

and why is sky a long breath out?
Why clouds the shape of getting lost?
Why thunder like an empty belly
round as a cloud and the sound of angry?

Why trees as still as empty afternoons
when I ask myself no questions?
Why sleep as creamy as a deep green sea
and fish with eyes like dreams?

Why sheep? Why the heavy wet rug
and the rumble of sheep
to lambs that bounce like surprises?
Why the other sheep: the wide-eyed head

the ribs like a wet piano
and all that red? And why the child?
Why did she come out
a mouth like a flower, open and wet;

a new rabbit with eyes like questions?
Why questions?
Why no still afternoons?
Why answers that leave her

hungry as thunder and cold as no fire
alone as a hole where there is no sky
empty as a mouth with no tongue in it
angry as a belly with no food in it.

No sun to warm it. No trees to still it.
No answers to fill it, why?

In the end

most of us still stuck to the rules, the left side of the road.
As a nation faced with the inevitable,
we remained mannered. We drove fast
but not without consideration – though we cursed
whichever farmer abandoned his tractor
in the single-lane track above Crosstones,
hurdling his own high dry-stone walls,
through his tussocks and flocks towards home.
Three minutes to go.

The sunlight was mellow as old water,
the sheep bemused by the uncharacteristic traffic,
bumper-to-bumper from Cliviger
back to my town, my old home,
where the toast still charred beneath the grill,
and the cat circled the empty rooms, looking for breakfast.
I regret now that I didn't feed her, didn't take
one greedy last look at the kettle, the sofa,
the bulbs erupting in pots at the door.
I miss it now, each rich inch of it

early morning, the mist still clearing,
the quiet town waiting for summer.
The old careful walls and the sheep.
At one minute left, I was sprinting towards family
with no hope of getting there in time.

Those were the hardest decisions to make –
which home to head for, which road to take.
And some of us took no decisions at all
but stood in the garden, at long last struck
by the mist on the hedge, the shivering grass,
the miraculous fact of the sky
or curled up so tight that our foreheads were scarred
by the mark of a kneecap, another person's face.
Notice I use the word *us*.

Then stop.
So far, this is all made up. What really concerns me
is this bad, last month's bad luck, the non-apocalyptic
suffering of friends. The personal catastrophes
of debt and insanity, the loss of a baby.
Three months in prison, a DSS caution
and beyond that, the blown-apart
buses and trains, the planes
in their thousand pieces. What I'm really saying is

in the end, we all turned to each other,
carried and held and helped each other,
gave what comfort we could to each other,
thrown over and over back to each other.
What I'm really saying is –
our ability to care for each other,
to stand with each other,
it's all that we have
in the end.

Gratitude

is what, at the end of it,
you are left with. Grateful for the fact
it was over, the sun continued to stream
through the leaves,

the sharp earth under your back.
For the afternoon's resumed silence,
the red-brick flats, the allotments,
the dry dirt track. How nothing dramatic

had changed. Grateful now
that you woke up this morning
feeling like death, the new abscess
under your tongue. For the washing-machine

which obliges you by spinning,
for the helpful kettle
and the sheets growing stiff on the line.
Suddenly glad to the point of tears

for tea-trays, for stars,
for your shoulders,
you write prayers to the God of flowerpots,
overcast days in July, old cats,

dead mice on the living-room carpet.
Grateful for the help you did not get,
the ungracious names you were given
as the price of surviving.

For morning coffee, growing older,
for people who try to do right by each other.
For the café, the weekday,
the night sky.

For your girlfriend's unpunctuated texts I LUV U RU OK
For young girls raped in the shade in July.

Grateful that you survived, most of all
grateful that you survived

PS
I AM OK

The soap opera inside me

is in big trouble.
It has strayed from its original roots,
the old stories are losing their way.
These days, no one knows what to expect –

there hasn't been a plane crash for several years;
the pubs and the corner-shops are intact,
the viaduct stands firm. As of late,
no one has torched the church

or even intends to.
Lesbians live at peace with their neighbours,
vicars, tax collectors. No one stares.
The boss buys a round for his workers

and there's no fighting, no spite,
no drunken backbiting.
It's almost frightening,
all this love

as the week spins brightly around a sunnier pivot
and even the backstreets are clean.
The newsagent gleams with good news,
and the butcher has given up meat.

The fields are white with undocked lambs
and by the canal,
rows of happy fishermen
content with no catching; one heron watching.

No wonder the rumours are spreading
that this soap is losing its thread – my God,
no one has died since Easter,
no nasty diseases, no wedding disasters.

Lined up for the happiest Christmas yet –
it's a tragedy waiting to happen,

a best set of china just bound to be broken
except

this soap has lost its original plot.
When the theme tune plays
there's a new voice behind the usual brass;
a new song. *Here comes the sun.*

After all these years of rain,
I can hardly sing along for laughing.
I can hardly read the credits
through the tears.

Bird

Years ago, when I was young enough
to eat mud and be interested
in stones and clocks and buried bones –
when I was that young,
I found a bird that couldn't fly.
I picked it up. Its chest was flecked

like the surface of a road;
its wing was blackened straw; its eye
was a kind of corridor.
You can ignore the panic of wild things.
They struggle because
they don't know better.

I put it in a box and dug for worms;
uprooted the seedlings my father had grown
all winter in his steamy plastic frames.
They were thin green sinews, fragile as ice.
I broke them, and was shouted at of course,
and only three sore worms
and a damp gum of a slug to show for it.

And the bird wouldn't eat.
The far hole of its eye was misted over
like a sick cat or a
great-great-grandmother.
A distance, comfortless as a spider.
You couldn't touch or stroke it.
It would sink lower

beneath the hollow shoulders
and the eye would echo emptier.
The jamlid of water grew a skin of dust and feathers
and the food crawled and soured.
The bird smelt sick, like bad music.
Like something broken,

a thing done wrong.

But one day I woke
and what came from its throat
was a firework of sound that flowered,
that ran like a river
over stones where fish shimmer.
Quick otters swam in the dark of its song.
Clouds bloomed, sky grew suddenly tall

and the room was yellow with morning.
It was the third day.
The cardboard was soggy as bread.
The bird was all bones. By noon, it was dead.
What am I trying to say?
Nothing.
It just happened. It just happened like I said.

www.ingramcontent.com/pod-product-compliance
Lightning Source LLC
Jackson TN
JSHW081321130125
77033JS00011B/392